EMMANUEL JOSEPH

The Green Chain, Billionaires, Crypto, and the Race to Save Nations and the Planet

Copyright © 2025 by Emmanuel Joseph

All rights reserved. No part of this publication may be reproduced, stored or transmitted in any form or by any means, electronic, mechanical, photocopying, recording, scanning, or otherwise without written permission from the publisher. It is illegal to copy this book, post it to a website, or distribute it by any other means without permission.

First edition

This book was professionally typeset on Reedsy.
Find out more at reedsy.com

Contents

1. Chapter 1: The Dawn of the Green Revolution — 1
2. Chapter 2: Crypto and the Environment — 3
3. Chapter 3: Billionaires with a Green Vision — 5
4. Chapter 4: The Intersection of Technology and Sustainability — 7
5. Chapter 5: Blockchain for Environmental Protection — 9
6. Chapter 6: Green Finance and Sustainable Investments — 11
7. Chapter 7: Decentralized Solutions for Climate Change — 13
8. Chapter 8: The Role of Governments and Policymakers — 15
9. Chapter 9: The Power of Collaboration — 17
10. Chapter 10: The Social Impact of the Green Revolution — 19
11. Chapter 11: The Future of Transportation — 21
12. Chapter 12: Renewable Energy and the Quest for Clean Power — 23
13. Chapter 13: The Circular Economy — 25
14. Chapter 14: Innovations in Agriculture and Food Systems — 27
15. Chapter 15: Resilience and Adaptation — 29
16. Chapter 16: Education and Awareness — 31
17. Chapter 17: The Path Forward — 33

1

Chapter 1: The Dawn of the Green Revolution

The 21st century witnessed an unprecedented fusion of technological innovation and environmental consciousness. As the world grappled with the escalating impacts of climate change, a new breed of entrepreneurs emerged, driven by a vision to marry profitability with sustainability. These visionaries recognized the potential of blockchain technology and cryptocurrencies to revolutionize the way we address environmental challenges. They saw beyond the traditional boundaries of business and finance, envisioning a future where technology could be harnessed for the greater good.

At the forefront of this green revolution were individuals who dared to dream big. They faced numerous challenges, from skepticism and regulatory hurdles to technological limitations. Yet, their unwavering commitment to their mission propelled them forward. This chapter introduces some of these pioneers, delving into their motivations, the obstacles they encountered, and the innovative solutions they devised to turn their ambitious ideas into reality.

The journey began with a deep understanding of the urgent need to combat climate change. These entrepreneurs were acutely aware of the environmental degradation caused by conventional industries. They sought to develop sustainable alternatives that would not only mitigate the negative impacts but also create new opportunities for growth and development. By leveraging the decentralized nature of blockchain and the transparency it offered, they aimed to build trust and accountability in their environmental initiatives.

One of the key turning points in this movement was the realization that collaboration was essential for success. The green revolution was not just about individual efforts but about building a collective force for change. These pioneers understood that working together with governments, non-profits, and the wider business community was crucial to achieving their goals. Their stories serve as a testament to the power of unity and the potential for transformative impact when diverse stakeholders come together for a common cause.

2

Chapter 2: Crypto and the Environment

Cryptocurrency, often associated with exorbitant energy consumption and environmental degradation, paradoxically became a cornerstone of the green revolution. The early years of Bitcoin mining painted a grim picture, with massive data centers guzzling electricity and leaving a substantial carbon footprint. However, technological advancements and a growing environmental consciousness within the crypto community began to shift this narrative.

Innovative approaches to mining emerged, driven by a desire to reduce the environmental impact of cryptocurrencies. Renewable energy-powered mining operations started to gain traction, with solar, wind, and hydroelectric power being harnessed to fuel the energy-intensive processes. This not only reduced the carbon footprint but also set a precedent for sustainable practices within the industry. The chapter explores how these renewable energy initiatives transformed the perception of cryptocurrencies, showcasing the efforts of key players who championed these changes.

Another significant development was the evolution of consensus mechanisms. The traditional proof-of-work (PoW) system, notorious for its energy consumption, gave way to more eco-friendly alternatives like proof-of-stake (PoS). PoS dramatically reduced the energy requirements for validating transactions, making it a more sustainable option. This chapter delves into the technical aspects of these mechanisms, highlighting how they contribute to the overall sustainability of the crypto ecosystem.

The narrative also touches upon the broader implications of these advancements. By addressing the environmental concerns associated with cryptocurrencies, the industry began to gain acceptance from a wider audience. This, in turn, opened up new avenues for blockchain technology to be applied in various environmental initiatives, from carbon credit trading to supply chain transparency. The chapter underscores the importance of continuous innovation and adaptation in making crypto a force for good in the fight against climate change.

3

Chapter 3: Billionaires with a Green Vision

In a world where wealth often equates to power, a select group of billionaires chose to wield their influence for the greater good. This chapter profiles these individuals, detailing their journeys from traditional business ventures to green investments. Their stories exemplify how financial success can be aligned with environmental stewardship, demonstrating that profitability and sustainability are not mutually exclusive.

Elon Musk, the enigmatic CEO of Tesla, is one such visionary. His pivot towards renewable energy with Tesla's electric vehicles (EVs) revolutionized the automotive industry. Musk's commitment to reducing carbon emissions extended beyond EVs to solar energy solutions and battery storage, making sustainable energy accessible to a broader audience. His relentless pursuit of innovation and willingness to challenge the status quo positioned him as a leading figure in the green revolution.

Another prominent billionaire, Bill Gates, channeled his resources into philanthropy through the Gates Foundation. Recognizing the interconnectedness of health, poverty, and the environment, Gates invested in sustainable agricultural practices, clean energy research, and climate resilience projects. His foundation's initiatives aimed to address the root causes of environmental degradation while improving the lives of marginalized communities. Gates' holistic approach to sustainability highlighted the need for integrated solutions to complex global challenges.

This chapter also features other influential figures like Jeff Bezos, who committed significant funds to combat climate change through the Bezos Earth Fund, and Richard Branson, whose ventures into renewable energy and sustainable tourism showcased the potential for green entrepreneurship. Their collective efforts underscore the transformative impact of aligning financial resources and expertise with a vision for a sustainable future.

4

Chapter 4: The Intersection of Technology and Sustainability

As the green revolution gained momentum, it became clear that the synergy between technology and sustainability was crucial for addressing the planet's most pressing challenges. This chapter examines the groundbreaking innovations at this intersection, from smart grids and energy-efficient buildings to AI-driven climate modeling. The integration of these technologies into everyday life paved the way for a more sustainable and resilient future.

Smart grids, for instance, revolutionized the way we generate, distribute, and consume energy. By leveraging advanced sensors and data analytics, smart grids optimized energy usage, reduced wastage, and facilitated the integration of renewable energy sources. This chapter explores the evolution of smart grid technology, highlighting successful implementations and their impact on reducing carbon emissions. The narrative also delves into the challenges of upgrading existing infrastructure and the role of policy frameworks in driving adoption.

Energy-efficient buildings emerged as another focal point in the quest for sustainability. Innovative designs and materials, coupled with smart technologies, transformed buildings into eco-friendly structures that minimized energy consumption and maximized resource efficiency. The chapter profiles pioneering projects and companies that led the way in green architecture, showcasing the potential for sustainable urban development. It also discusses the importance of retrofitting existing buildings to meet modern energy standards, emphasizing the role of collaboration between architects, engineers, and policymakers.

AI-driven climate modeling offered unprecedented insights into the complexities of climate change. Advanced algorithms and machine learning techniques enabled scientists to analyze vast amounts of data, predict future trends, and devise effective mitigation strategies. This chapter explores the applications of AI in climate research, from monitoring deforestation and glacier melt to optimizing renewable energy deployment. The narrative underscores the importance of data-driven decision-making in addressing environmental challenges and highlights the potential of AI to revolutionize our understanding of the natural world.

By examining these technological advancements, this chapter paints a vivid picture of how innovation is paving the way for a sustainable future. It emphasizes the need for continuous investment in research and development, as well as the importance of fostering a culture of collaboration and knowledge sharing to drive meaningful progress in the green revolution.

5

Chapter 5: Blockchain for Environmental Protection

Blockchain technology, with its decentralized and immutable nature, emerged as a powerful tool for environmental protection. As industries and governments increasingly recognized the potential of blockchain, a myriad of applications began to surface, each aiming to address specific environmental challenges. One of the most impactful applications was the use of blockchain for carbon credit trading. By leveraging the transparency and traceability of blockchain, carbon credits could be accurately tracked and traded, ensuring that emissions reductions were genuine and accounted for.

Another innovative application of blockchain was in supply chain transparency. Companies began to use blockchain to trace the origins of raw materials and products, ensuring that they were sourced sustainably and ethically. This not only helped reduce the environmental footprint of supply chains but also built trust with consumers who were increasingly demanding transparency. The chapter delves into case studies of companies that successfully implemented blockchain-based supply chain solutions, highlighting the benefits and challenges they encountered.

Anti-poaching efforts also saw a significant boost from blockchain technology. By using blockchain to track and verify the movement of endangered species, conservationists were able to combat illegal wildlife trade more effectively. This chapter explores how blockchain projects have made a tangible impact on wildlife conservation, showcasing the potential of this technology to drive positive environmental outcomes. The narrative underscores the importance of collaboration between technologists, environmentalists, and policymakers in harnessing the full potential of blockchain for the planet's benefit.

6

Chapter 6: Green Finance and Sustainable Investments

The rise of green finance marked a turning point in the fight against climate change. As the world began to recognize the economic risks of environmental degradation, investors started to shift their focus towards sustainable projects. Green bonds, a form of debt instrument specifically earmarked for climate and environmental projects, gained popularity among investors seeking both financial returns and positive environmental impact.

Impact investing emerged as another key component of the green finance ecosystem. This investment strategy sought to generate measurable social and environmental benefits alongside financial returns. By channeling capital towards projects that addressed issues such as clean energy, sustainable agriculture, and affordable housing, impact investors played a crucial role in driving the green revolution. This chapter profiles leading financial institutions and investment funds that have embraced sustainability as a core principle, highlighting their contributions to the global green economy.

Environmental, Social, and Governance (ESG) criteria became a fundamental consideration for investors and companies alike. By evaluating investments based on their ESG performance, investors were able to identify companies that were committed to sustainable practices. This chapter explores the evolution of ESG investing, discussing the challenges and opportunities in integrating ESG criteria into mainstream investment strategies. The narrative also delves into the role of regulatory frameworks and market incentives in promoting green finance, emphasizing the need for a holistic approach to sustainable investments.

7

Chapter 7: Decentralized Solutions for Climate Change

Decentralization, a fundamental principle of blockchain technology, found new applications in the battle against climate change. By empowering local communities and individuals to take collective action, decentralized solutions fostered a sense of ownership and responsibility towards the environment. Community-led renewable energy projects, for instance, allowed neighborhoods to generate and manage their own clean energy, reducing their reliance on fossil fuels and enhancing energy resilience.

Decentralized environmental monitoring networks emerged as another innovative application. By leveraging blockchain and IoT (Internet of Things) technology, these networks enabled real-time monitoring of environmental conditions, such as air and water quality. This decentralized approach to data collection and analysis provided valuable insights for policymakers and environmentalists, facilitating more effective and targeted interventions. The chapter explores successful implementations of decentralized environmental monitoring, highlighting the benefits of community-driven initiatives.

Decentralized Autonomous Organizations (DAOs) also showed promise in coordinating large-scale environmental initiatives. By using blockchain-based smart contracts, DAOs enabled transparent and efficient decision-making processes, ensuring that resources were allocated effectively. This chapter delves into the potential of DAOs in managing environmental projects, from reforestation efforts to plastic waste cleanup. The narrative emphasizes the importance of decentralization in fostering collaboration and innovation, ultimately driving progress in the fight against climate change.

8

Chapter 8: The Role of Governments and Policymakers

While the private sector played a crucial role in the green revolution, the support and involvement of governments and policymakers were indispensable. This chapter examines the policies and regulations that enabled the growth of green technologies and sustainable practices. International agreements such as the Paris Agreement set the stage for global cooperation on climate action, committing countries to reduce their greenhouse gas emissions and limit global warming.

National and local initiatives further supported the transition to a sustainable future. Governments introduced incentives such as tax credits, grants, and subsidies to promote renewable energy adoption, energy efficiency, and sustainable transportation. Regulatory frameworks aimed to reduce emissions, enhance environmental protection, and encourage innovation. This chapter explores the impact of these policies on the green revolution, highlighting successful case studies from around the world.

The narrative also delves into the challenges of aligning the interests of the public and private sectors. Policymakers faced the task of balancing economic growth with environmental sustainability, navigating complex political landscapes, and addressing the concerns of various stakeholders. The chapter emphasizes the importance of collaboration between governments, businesses, and civil society in achieving common environmental goals. By working together, these diverse actors could create a supportive ecosystem for green innovation and drive meaningful progress towards a sustainable future.

9

Chapter 9: The Power of Collaboration

In the race to save the planet, collaboration emerged as a key driver of progress. The complex and multifaceted nature of environmental challenges required diverse expertise and resources, making partnerships essential. This chapter highlights the importance of collaboration between businesses, governments, non-profits, and academia in driving the green revolution.

One of the most successful examples of collaboration is the Global Alliance for Climate Solutions, a coalition of organizations from different sectors working together to address climate change. By pooling their resources and expertise, these organizations have implemented large-scale projects that have significantly reduced greenhouse gas emissions and promoted sustainable practices. The chapter explores the structure and strategies of the alliance, showcasing the impact of their collective efforts on a global scale.

Another notable example is the collaboration between tech companies and environmental NGOs. Companies like Microsoft and Google have partnered with organizations such as the World Wildlife Fund and The Nature Conservancy to develop innovative solutions for conservation and sustainability. These partnerships have resulted in the creation of advanced tools for environmental monitoring, data analysis, and resource management. The chapter delves into specific projects and initiatives, highlighting the benefits of leveraging technology for environmental protection.

The narrative also emphasizes the role of community-driven initiatives in fostering collaboration. Local communities, often at the forefront of environmental challenges, have developed grassroots solutions that address their unique needs and circumstances. By partnering with local governments, non-profits, and businesses, these communities have successfully implemented projects that promote sustainability and resilience. The chapter showcases inspiring stories of community-led initiatives, emphasizing the importance of empowering individuals and groups to take collective action.

10

Chapter 10: The Social Impact of the Green Revolution

The green revolution extended beyond environmental sustainability to encompass social and economic dimensions. The transition to a sustainable future brought about significant changes in various aspects of society, from job creation and community empowerment to social equity and justice. This chapter explores the social impact of green technologies and practices, highlighting initiatives that have improved the livelihoods of marginalized communities and fostered inclusive economic growth.

One of the most profound social impacts of the green revolution is the creation of green jobs. As industries shifted towards sustainable practices, new employment opportunities emerged in sectors such as renewable energy, energy efficiency, and sustainable agriculture. This chapter delves into the role of green jobs in driving economic growth and reducing unemployment, particularly in regions that have been disproportionately affected by environmental degradation. The narrative also discusses the importance of providing education and training programs to equip workers with the skills needed for the green economy.

Community empowerment is another key aspect of the green revolution's social impact. By involving local communities in environmental initiatives, projects have fostered a sense of ownership and responsibility towards the environment. This chapter explores case studies of community-led projects that have improved living conditions, enhanced resilience to climate change, and promoted social cohesion. The narrative emphasizes the importance of inclusive decision-making processes and the need to address social inequalities in the pursuit of sustainability.

Social equity and justice are fundamental principles of the green revolution. The chapter discusses initiatives that have aimed to address the disproportionate impacts of environmental degradation on marginalized communities. From access to clean energy and water to affordable housing and transportation, these initiatives have sought to ensure that the benefits of sustainability are equitably distributed. The narrative underscores the interconnectedness of environmental and social issues, advocating for holistic approaches to sustainable development that prioritize the well-being of all individuals and communities.

11

Chapter 11: The Future of Transportation

The transportation sector, a major contributor to greenhouse gas emissions, underwent a radical transformation during the green revolution. Innovations in transportation technology and infrastructure reshaped the way people and goods moved, paving the way for a more sustainable and efficient future. This chapter examines the advancements that revolutionized the transportation sector, from electric and hydrogen-powered vehicles to autonomous and shared mobility solutions.

Electric vehicles (EVs) became a cornerstone of the green transportation revolution. With advancements in battery technology and charging infrastructure, EVs offered a viable alternative to fossil fuel-powered vehicles. This chapter explores the development and adoption of EVs, highlighting the efforts of companies like Tesla, Nissan, and BYD in driving the transition to electric mobility. The narrative also discusses the challenges and opportunities in achieving widespread adoption, including the need for supportive policies and incentives.

Hydrogen-powered vehicles emerged as another promising solution for sustainable transportation. By using hydrogen fuel cells to generate electricity, these vehicles produced zero emissions and offered longer ranges than traditional EVs. The chapter delves into the advancements in hydrogen technology, showcasing successful implementations in buses, trucks, and trains. The narrative also explores the potential of hydrogen as a clean energy source for various sectors beyond transportation.

Autonomous and shared mobility solutions further transformed the transportation landscape. Autonomous vehicles (AVs) promised to enhance safety, reduce traffic congestion, and improve fuel efficiency. Shared mobility services, such as ride-sharing and bike-sharing, offered convenient and eco-friendly alternatives to private car ownership. This chapter examines the integration of these technologies into urban transportation systems, highlighting pilot projects and successful case studies. The narrative emphasizes the role of smart infrastructure and urban planning in creating sustainable transportation networks that cater to the needs of diverse populations.

12

Chapter 12: Renewable Energy and the Quest for Clean Power

Renewable energy sources, such as solar, wind, and hydroelectric power, became the cornerstone of the green revolution. As the world sought to reduce its reliance on fossil fuels and transition to clean energy, significant advancements in renewable energy technologies and infrastructure were made. This chapter delves into the developments that transformed the global energy landscape and accelerated the shift towards a sustainable future.

Solar energy emerged as one of the most promising renewable energy sources. Advancements in photovoltaic technology and reductions in production costs made solar power more accessible and affordable. This chapter explores the growth of the solar industry, highlighting large-scale solar projects, innovative applications, and the role of supportive policies in driving adoption. The narrative also discusses the challenges of integrating solar energy into the grid, such as intermittency and storage, and the solutions developed to address these issues.

Wind energy also played a crucial role in the renewable energy transition. The development of larger and more efficient wind turbines, along with advancements in offshore wind technology, expanded the potential for wind power generation. This chapter examines the growth of the wind energy sector, showcasing successful projects and the benefits of wind power in terms of energy generation and job creation. The narrative also explores the environmental and social considerations of wind energy development, such as habitat conservation and community engagement.

Hydroelectric power, a well-established renewable energy source, continued to contribute significantly to the global energy mix. This chapter explores the innovations in hydroelectric technology, such as small-scale and run-of-river systems, that enhanced the sustainability and efficiency of hydroelectric power generation. The narrative also delves into the environmental and social impacts of large-scale hydroelectric projects, emphasizing the importance of balancing energy production with ecosystem preservation and community well-being.

By examining these renewable energy advancements, this chapter paints a comprehensive picture of the quest for clean power. It emphasizes the need for continued investment in research and development, as well as the importance of supportive policies and market incentives in accelerating the renewable energy transition. The narrative also underscores the interconnectedness of renewable energy with other aspects of the green revolution, such as transportation, finance, and technology.

13

Chapter 13: The Circular Economy

The concept of the circular economy, which aims to minimize waste and maximize resource efficiency, gained prominence during the green revolution. This chapter explores the principles and practices of the circular economy, highlighting how it transforms traditional linear production models into closed-loop systems. The shift towards a circular economy requires rethinking how products are designed, manufactured, used, and disposed of, with the goal of extending their lifecycle and reducing environmental impact.

One of the fundamental principles of the circular economy is designing for longevity and recyclability. By creating products that are durable, easy to repair, and made from recyclable materials, businesses can reduce the need for raw materials and minimize waste. This chapter delves into the innovative design approaches adopted by companies, showcasing successful examples of products that embody circular economy principles. The narrative also discusses the role of product stewardship and extended producer responsibility in promoting sustainable design.

Recycling and upcycling are essential components of the circular economy. By converting waste materials into new products, these practices help conserve resources and reduce the environmental footprint of production. This chapter explores the advancements in recycling technology, such as chemical recycling and automated sorting systems, that have enhanced the efficiency and effectiveness of recycling processes. The narrative also highlights creative upcycling projects that turn waste into valuable products, emphasizing the potential for innovation in resource recovery.

Another critical aspect of the circular economy is the transition from ownership to access-based business models. By offering products as services, companies can reduce resource consumption and encourage more sustainable consumption patterns. This chapter examines the rise of the sharing economy, from car-sharing and tool libraries to subscription-based models for clothing and electronics. The narrative explores the benefits and challenges of these models, emphasizing the need for consumer education and behavioral change to drive their adoption.

14

Chapter 14: Innovations in Agriculture and Food Systems

Agriculture, a critical sector for both food security and environmental sustainability, underwent significant transformation during the green revolution. This chapter examines the innovations in sustainable agriculture and food systems that have enhanced productivity while minimizing environmental impact. From precision farming and regenerative agriculture to plant-based and lab-grown foods, these advancements are reshaping the future of food production.

Precision farming, which uses data-driven technologies to optimize agricultural practices, has revolutionized the way farmers manage their crops and livestock. By leveraging tools such as GPS, sensors, and drones, farmers can monitor soil health, water usage, and crop growth in real-time, allowing for more efficient and sustainable resource management. This chapter delves into the applications of precision farming, showcasing successful implementations and their impact on reducing inputs and improving yields.

Regenerative agriculture, which focuses on restoring and enhancing soil health, has gained traction as a sustainable farming practice. By employing techniques such as cover cropping, crop rotation, and agroforestry, regenerative agriculture aims to build soil organic matter, increase biodiversity, and sequester carbon. This chapter explores the principles and benefits of regenerative agriculture, highlighting case studies of farms that have successfully transitioned to these practices. The narrative also discusses the role of policy support and market incentives in promoting regenerative agriculture.

The development of plant-based and lab-grown foods represents a significant innovation in addressing the environmental impact of traditional animal agriculture. By creating alternatives to meat and dairy products, these technologies offer a more sustainable way to meet the growing demand for protein. This chapter examines the advancements in plant-based protein sources, such as soy, pea, and mycoprotein, as well as the breakthroughs in cellular agriculture that have enabled the production of lab-grown meat. The narrative explores the potential of these innovations to reduce greenhouse gas emissions, land use, and water consumption associated with conventional animal farming.

15

Chapter 15: Resilience and Adaptation

As the impacts of climate change became increasingly evident, resilience and adaptation emerged as crucial components of the green revolution. Building resilience to climate-related risks and enhancing adaptive capacity are essential for ensuring the sustainability and well-being of communities and ecosystems. This chapter explores the strategies and initiatives aimed at strengthening resilience and adaptation in the face of climate change.

Infrastructure design and urban planning play a vital role in building climate resilience. By incorporating climate-resilient features such as green roofs, permeable pavements, and natural flood defenses, cities can better withstand the impacts of extreme weather events. This chapter examines innovative approaches to urban planning that enhance resilience, showcasing successful examples of climate-resilient infrastructure projects. The narrative also discusses the importance of integrating climate considerations into all aspects of urban development, from zoning and building codes to transportation and energy systems.

Ecosystem restoration is another critical strategy for enhancing resilience and adaptation. Healthy ecosystems, such as forests, wetlands, and coral reefs, provide essential services that help mitigate the impacts of climate change, such as carbon sequestration, water purification, and coastal protection. This chapter explores the efforts to restore and conserve ecosystems, highlighting successful restoration projects and their benefits for both the environment and local communities. The narrative also emphasizes the need for community involvement and participatory approaches in ecosystem restoration initiatives.

Community-based adaptation (CBA) is a bottom-up approach that empowers communities to identify and implement adaptation strategies tailored to their specific needs and contexts. By involving local stakeholders in the decision-making process, CBA ensures that adaptation measures are culturally appropriate, socially inclusive, and economically viable. This chapter delves into the principles and practices of CBA, showcasing case studies of communities that have successfully enhanced their resilience to climate change. The narrative also discusses the challenges and opportunities in scaling up CBA efforts and integrating them into broader adaptation frameworks.

16

Chapter 16: Education and Awareness

Education and awareness are pivotal in fostering a culture of sustainability and environmental stewardship. By raising public awareness about climate change and promoting environmental education at all levels, individuals can be empowered to make informed decisions and take meaningful action. This chapter examines the efforts to enhance education and awareness, highlighting the role of schools, universities, media, and grassroots organizations in shaping environmental attitudes and behaviors.

Environmental education in schools and universities is crucial for equipping the next generation with the knowledge and skills needed to address environmental challenges. This chapter explores innovative approaches to environmental education, such as experiential learning, project-based learning, and interdisciplinary curricula. The narrative highlights successful programs and initiatives that have integrated sustainability into educational institutions, emphasizing the importance of fostering critical thinking, problem-solving, and collaborative skills.

Media and communication play a significant role in raising public awareness and shaping perceptions of environmental issues. By leveraging traditional media, social media, and digital platforms, environmental advocates can reach diverse audiences and inspire action. This chapter delves into the strategies and campaigns that have successfully raised awareness about climate change and sustainability, showcasing the power of storytelling and visual communication. The narrative also discusses the challenges of combating misinformation and promoting accurate and balanced coverage of environmental topics.

Grassroots organizations and community groups are essential drivers of environmental awareness and action at the local level. By organizing events, workshops, and campaigns, these groups engage and mobilize individuals to take collective action. This chapter explores the efforts of grassroots organizations in promoting environmental education and awareness, highlighting inspiring examples of community-led initiatives. The narrative emphasizes the importance of building local networks and fostering a sense of community and shared responsibility in the pursuit of sustainability.

17

Chapter 17: The Path Forward

The green revolution marked the beginning of a new era in the quest to save nations and the planet. While significant progress has been made, the journey towards a sustainable and equitable future is ongoing. This chapter reflects on the achievements of the green revolution, the lessons learned, and the challenges that lie ahead. It emphasizes the need for sustained commitment, innovation, and collaboration to continue driving positive change.

The narrative highlights the importance of maintaining momentum and building on the successes of the green revolution. By fostering a culture of continuous improvement and learning, individuals, businesses, governments, and communities can adapt to evolving challenges and seize new opportunities. This chapter discusses the role of innovation in driving sustainable solutions, from technological advancements to policy and market innovations. It emphasizes the need for ongoing research and development, investment in sustainable technologies, and the creation of supportive policy frameworks.

Collaboration remains a cornerstone of the path forward. By strengthening partnerships and fostering cross-sectoral cooperation, diverse stakeholders can leverage their collective expertise and resources to address complex environmental challenges. This chapter explores the potential of global networks and alliances in sharing knowledge, resources, and best practices, emphasizing the importance of inclusivity and diversity in collaborative efforts.

The narrative concludes with a call to action, urging individuals, businesses, governments, and communities to continue striving for a greener, healthier, and more resilient world. It emphasizes the interconnectedness of environmental, social, and economic issues, advocating for holistic approaches to sustainable development. The chapter also underscores the importance of hope, resilience, and determination in the face of adversity, inspiring readers to take meaningful action and contribute to the ongoing journey towards a sustainable future.

The Green Chain: Billionaires, Crypto, and the Race to Save Nations and the Planet

In a world on the brink of environmental catastrophe, the green revolution has begun, driven by an unlikely alliance of billionaire entrepreneurs, cutting-edge blockchain technology, and an urgent need for sustainable solutions. "The Green Chain" takes readers on a compelling journey through the convergence of wealth, innovation, and environmental consciousness.

This book delves into the remarkable stories of visionaries who dared to dream beyond conventional boundaries, harnessing the power of cryptocurrencies and blockchain to create a sustainable future. From Elon Musk's quest to revolutionize energy with Tesla to Bill Gates' philanthropic initiatives addressing global challenges, these billionaires wield their influence for the greater good.

Explore the transformative impact of green finance, where sustainable investments and green bonds pave the way for a new economic paradigm. Witness the rise of decentralized solutions that empower local communities to take collective action against climate change. Discover how technology and sustainability intersect in groundbreaking innovations, from smart grids and energy-efficient buildings to AI-driven climate modeling.

"The Green Chain" also highlights the social dimension of the green revolution, showcasing initiatives that create green jobs, empower communities, and promote social equity. Learn about the future of transportation with electric, hydrogen-powered, and autonomous vehicles, and the quest for clean power through advancements in solar, wind, and hydroelectric energy.

Embrace the principles of the circular economy, transforming waste into valuable resources and rethinking consumption patterns. Dive into the world of sustainable agriculture and food systems, where precision farming, regenerative practices, and plant-based foods reshape the way we produce and consume food.

As the journey unfolds, "The Green Chain" emphasizes the importance of resilience and adaptation in the face of climate change, the role of education and awareness in fostering a culture of sustainability, and the power of collaboration in driving meaningful progress.

This book serves as a call to action, urging individuals, businesses, governments, and communities to continue striving for a greener, healthier, and more resilient world. "The Green Chain" is a testament to the transformative potential of aligning financial success with environmental stewardship, inspiring readers to be part of the ongoing quest to save our planet.

www.ingramcontent.com/pod-product-compliance
Lightning Source LLC
LaVergne TN
LVHW020459080526
838202LV00057B/6036